The *change*

Luang Phaw Dhammajayo

Copyright © 2007 Tawandhamma Foundation

First published in 2007 by:
Tawandhamma Foundation
P. O. Box 122
Khlong Luang District
Pathumthani Province
THAILAND 12120
info@tawandhamma.org
www.tawandhamma.org

Edited & Designed by:
The Print Lodge Pte Ltd
16 Arumugam Road
#03-04 Lion Building D
Singapore 409961
info@theprintlodge.com.sg

ISBN: 978-981-05-7757-5 (Singapore)

Printed in Singapore

to

All Mankind Who Will
Change the World
Peacefully

Foreword

We all wish we live in a better world
Some believe war is the mighty way
Only to find victory sours to revenge
And misery, so we doubt
True peace can ever be
Awards and rewards we present
But greed and hatred seem more dominant
Let us return to the simple way
That people of all ages can obey
Our wish may yet come true
Such a simple thing to do
To close our eyes and relax through and through
To still your mind at the centre
Until cool brightness freshens you
Encircling with the best of happiness
Blessing others with love and kindness
Conflict and difference then dissolve
Tomorrow the world will evolve
Changing through this simple way
A secret I share with all of humanity.

Luang Phaw Dhammajayo
1 July 2006

Introduction

Peace. This is a word all of us know. We have heard it spoken countless of times in the media by politicians, but it is a word rarely uttered by common people. It is as if the notion of peace is far removed from our day to day existence. For most people today, 'peace' conjures the image of an international conference centre with hundreds of national flags fluttering in orderly rows, with sombre leaders and representatives of countries, all dressed in formal attire, delivering impressive speeches under a spotlight and shaking hands on the world stage to reverberating applause. We take for granted that the process of achieving world peace must follow the channels of politics, international compromises and signed treaties. We think that peace is the responsibility of world-class organisations like the United Nations, national governments and non-governmental organisations. We have come to believe that creating peace is not our duty but the domain of someone else who has power, holds a governing position, has budgets, and is somehow more organised than the average citizen. So our home is left to endure wars and political, economic and religious conflicts. Establishing world peace seems as unattainable as catching shadows in one's hand. The dream of global happiness seems to deteriorate with the news of each bomb explosion, each person senselessly killed, each hateful word uttered.

Although peace is profoundly complex and deeply important to all humanity, let us define it simply for now as a sense of happiness and well-being. Indeed, peace can exist everywhere – within your heart, your family, your neighbourhood, your society and nation; even encompassing the entire world. The term 'world peace', then, can be generalised as 'the world's happiness' in which everyone on the planet experiences and shares this sense of contentment. We all long for it, yet a vast majority of us have not realised that we are the most significant and essential element in which peace can flourish. Changing this world into a place of true peace is the responsibility of all of us. Born as intelligent beings who inhabit this earth, are we then not responsible for world peace – a happiness belonging to the world as well as to ourselves? We cannot claim that peace-making is the work of the others.

In concert with the efforts made by national governments, organisations and dedicated individuals who tirelessly seek ways to cure the ills of wars and conflicts through technology and strategies, Luang Phaw Dhammajayo, the Most Venerable Phrarajbhavanavisudh, the abbot of Dhammakaya Temple and president of Dhammakaya Foundation, offers his distinctive solution. Ordained since 1969, he is dedicated to immersing himself in the study and practice of the Buddha's pure teachings. For almost 40 years, he has always emphasised to the thousands of those who follow his teachings at the Dhammakaya Temple, branch centres and homes worldwide that "world peace needs to stem from inner peace".

"Everyone has an important role to play in changing this world for the betterment of humanity. Although the task is difficult, it can be attained through a method so simple that it is often overlooked".

Luang Phaw Dhammajayo's teachings are not merely based on an ideal concept shaped by philosophical thoughts. His teachings are truths of life that he had experimented upon and proved to be true by his own practice, and corroborated by the experience of others. This path brings about great willpower to abstain from bad deeds and to practice good deeds, as well as to keep one's mind pure and energetic. He has been successful in conveying these practices to his students so that they may change and improve themselves. Practitioners of his method, who attained inner happiness, have themselves become beacons of kindness and peace in their families and communities. They are capable of banishing dark thoughts that taint their minds and they share their happiness with others. These testimonies from people from all walks of life prove that Luang Phaw Dhammajayo's guidance is capable of transforming lives for the better – for the individual, the family and society and the world at large – bringing about a movement towards peace in a non-violent, non-political way.

On the occasion of Luang Phaw Dhammajayo's nomination for the Mahatma Gandhi Peace Award from the All Indian Gandhian Worker Society in India in 2005, the Universal Peace Award from World Buddhist Sangha Youth in Sri Lanka in 2006 and the Atish Dipankar Peace Gold Award from the Bangladesh Bouddha Kristi Prachar Sangha in 2007, I, with dedicated students across the globe, would like to take this opportunity to express our delight in compiling his valuable teachings into this book. Our hope is to share our pursuit of peace with the countless peace-seekers of the world who long to create better lives for themselves, their families, society, nations and the whole world.

May the teachings in this book give you the knowledge and strength to attain inner joy and to become a champion of peace on earth. May peace prevail on earth forever.

Anant. Asavabhokhin.

Mr. Anant Asavabhokhin
On behalf of the Publication Committee and Luang Phaw's disciples worldwide

Best CEO of the Year, 2004
Star of Asia, 2003
President of the Building Committee for the Dhammakaya Cetiya

3 March 2007

Contents

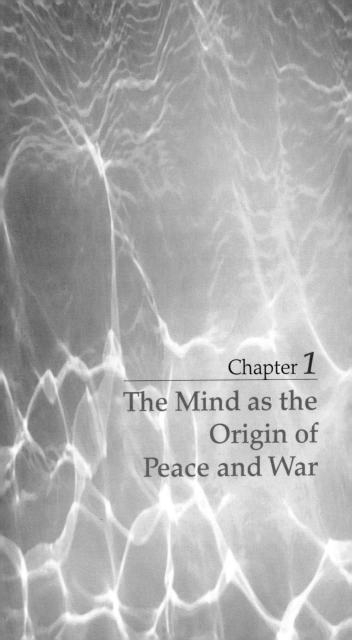

Chapter *1*
The Mind as the Origin of Peace and War

The human experience is composed of two important parts, the body and the mind. These two elements communicate back and forth with each other from the moment of birth until death. We recognise the fact that the conscious mind controls how we think, speak and act in most situations. Sometimes these actions are admirable, even noble, but at other times they can be shameful. For this very reason, our minds can be the starting point for both war and peace in the world. If a person's mind is infected by greed, anger and ignorance, thoughts that lead to conflicts arise. Like the flame of a tiny matchstick that is capable of completely consuming houses and even cities, all the wars and strife happening across the world, causing enormous suffering for millions of people, are ignited by a flame within the mind.

Just as the mind can be the source of suffering, a calm and aware mind can be the wellspring of wisdom, peace and infinite happiness that will envelop the individual, his family, the community, society and all the people of the world. From this beginning, world peace can happen – once we realise that the mind is an important instrument that can spark wars or perpetuate peace.

Throughout history, we have fought one another, whether on a large scale like World War I and World War II, on a smaller scale such as civil wars, or as confrontation between individuals. The human race has never once stopped fighting. While we sleep at night, on the other side of the world where there is sunlight, conflicts are constantly taking place between nations and between individuals. When it is daylight for us and the other side of the world is blanketed in darkness, we reverse roles in a cycle of endless killing and violence.

These never-ending wars and battles originate from clouded and misguided minds of people. In some instances, the people who initiated war will reason that they are really fighting to establish peace. The truth of the matter is that war causes physical and psychological damage, more suffering and death. To argue that war brings peace is to argue that the best way to put out a fire is to douse it with a bucket of gasoline. Wars only serve to fuel the hostility and hatred between the combatants and multiply the atrocities – moving the possibility of peace even further away from our grasp.

Worldly conflicts have never been able to bring lasting happiness to anyone. The victorious may one day be defeated. The conquered, instead of accepting defeat, allow resentment and revenge to fester in their hearts. Mutual distrust and hatred bind the conqueror and the conquered together in misery long after the actual war is over, and both sides will suffer the consequences of their hostility, generation after generation.

In some countries, people live in dread under the constant threat of terrorism. Never knowing when the next attack may take place, they are neither happy nor secure. To eliminate this constant threat of attack, they strike preemptively at their perceived enemies. Instead of reprieve, they find themselves at the centre of a cycle of revenge, with consequences that are more dire than they can understand because what they fail to comprehend is how long the hatred and malice, caused by their actions, will perpetuate in the hearts of millions of people. History has demonstrated that instead of peace, wars only beget great pain, planting the roots of suffering and hatred deeply into the bodies and minds of everyone involved.

If we can reflect with a mind devoid of any ill bias, we will come to realise that all people are our siblings. We breathe the same air. We drink water from the same rain clouds. We gaze upon the same sun, moon and stars. We inhabit the same earth from birth, until the last seconds of our lives. We all must endure the process of suffering, birth, aging and death. We all are slaves to evil which seizes every opportunity to invade our minds in times of weakness. We all live under the law of karma. With so much in common, we should not be fighting each other since we were never enemies to begin with.

It is a great tragedy that humanity wastes its time and resources on physical wars. Instead, we should place greater importance on waging the war within us because it is a conflict with more lasting consequences than anyone has ever imagined. The enemy is not another human being, but the inner demons of greed, anger, ignorance and all the different defilements that reside in each of us. These are the true enemies of humanity. In every step of this fight, there is no physical loss of life or limb. No one sheds tears, feels sorrow or harbours resentment. Instead, there is only joy in this battle, one that is vital in creating an enduring world peace.

We can initiate the inner 'war' by focusing our minds on our calm centre. Just as a doctor seeks the root of disease using microscopes with powerful magnifications, we can see and understand complex issues that require an above-normal comprehension with a focused and clear mind. If we can train the mind to its highest potential, we will see with clarity, the true enemy – defilement – embedded deep inside our minds, the source behind all suffering, conflicts and strife in the world. Powerful and ingrained as it is, you can eliminate this enemy just by calming the mind. It is a technique to collect and focus the purity of the mind in order to completely eradicate what is impure.

When you are able to defeat the defilements, you become a light that will guide your life and those of others close to you to the final destination in warmth and safety. When people from all corners of the world are able to do this, it will be like a million candles shining their light to banish the darkness that currently overshadows us. When we destroy the causes of war – greed, ignorance and anger – we also eliminate their consequences. This is the way to create true and enduring freedom and world peace.

Chapter 2
The Common Human Goal

Our world does not consist of only those who are warmongers; there are also those who have a strong determination to create a peaceful world. Some are working independently, but many have joined and formed organisations to discuss and exchange ideas on ways to promote world peace. These discussions, with peace as a common goal, have taken place numerous times among the world's different organisations. Such organisations have invested great amounts of time, money and effort at meetings and conferences to promote love and unity between different nations. They have also awarded annual peace prizes to raise awareness as well as to acknowledge the efforts of those who continue to make world peace their life's work.

While we must admire and applaud the dedication of those who pursue peace, the truth is that real world peace has not yet been attained. Wars and battles continue to be waged without end. True world peace has not taken place because we have failed to tackle the cause at its deepest roots. We still do not understand what peace really is, where it can be found, and how to plant it and encourage it to flourish.

Even though humankind comprise of people of different races, languages, religions, cultures and traditions, we have in common the long search for true happiness and the meaning of life, which are commendable aspirations. But what is peace and happiness, and from where do they originate? If we do not know the answer to these questions, how then can we attain peace and happiness? Since we do not know, we continue to pursue these aspirations based on our own wisdom and insights. However, if our wisdom is not fully developed, then our pursuit becomes random and unorganised, making achievement of that peace we are seeking haphazard at best. With such an imperfect understanding of our goals, we may as well seek water from rocks or fish in the desert.

We have to realise that while peace efforts such as international conferences among national leaders, award presentations and community projects can help to create a peaceful world partially, true world peace can only take place when everyone takes part by following the path to attaining inner peace. Every single person who does so is a true hero deserving of the most honourable peace award. If we can get every leader of every nation to start practicing meditation so that they too may experience and understand inner peace, we can quickly change the course of this world to a more peaceful one.

Chapter 3
Religions for Peace

Our global community is comprised of people seeking refuge in various faiths. For the most part, the founder of each religion – be it Buddhism, Christianity, Islam, Hindu, Sikh or other religions – has taught us to love our fellow humankind. If we continue to exploit, kill, cheat and injure one another, we are not adhering to the teachings of our respective religions. We no longer seek the peace that our religions have taught us to pursue.

Throughout history, some have tried to use religion as a tool to disunite humanity. These people hold false understanding that people of other faiths are enemies and are competitors that are to be defeated. They propagate misunderstanding and proclaim that religious differences have made us unable to live together in harmony. All who love their religion should study their original religious teachings. Buddhists should study the original teachings of Lord Buddha. Christians, Jews and Muslims should study the original teachings of their religion. Perhaps then, each will see that the original message of each religion is that of love and respect for all living things that they can correctly practice in their everyday lives. If we all do so, we close the path to grief and open the door to joy and heaven. If we love our fellow humankind, we must not kill or harm one another, but rather, dedicate ourselves to living together peacefully.

We must remember that, although the path to attaining peace differs according to one's knowledge, understanding, culture, tradition, attitude and personal satisfaction, every religion was formed to guide people with a philosophy to live happily. In reality the true common enemy for all humankind is our defilement, which includes greed, anger and ignorance. The defilement in our minds is the true cause of conflicts, not religion. Such defilements lead us to think, speak and act in cruel, aggressive and intolerant ways that lead to pain and suffering in this world. Reject your defilements. Understand that regardless of your religion, people of different faiths do not need to despise or kill one another when what all of us want fundamentally is to live in contentment and peace.

Chapter 4

World Peace through Inner Peace

Men who seek peace have long debated how world peace should begin. They examine diverse environmental factors such as ecology, food supply, medicine access, laws, nuclear weapons limitation, treaties, technology, political stability, the economy, society and poverty. Despite such close and detailed examination, they fail to notice that the origin of peace is much more intimate than any of those factors they have studied. The starting point of peace is within them.

The dream of world peace will never come true if the dreamer is unable to find his or her own inner contentment. Once everyone experiences inner happiness, true world peace will occur. When the defilements in the hearts of humankind are totally eliminated, things that were once beyond our imagination, like world peace, are suddenly possible and within reach. All it takes is to accomplish that first step – which is to practice meditation to experience the source of inner happiness. This knowledge is as ancient as the human race.

Happiness from within can be attained by quietly stilling the mind at the centre of one's body. The deeper you sink into this peace and calm found at the centre of each of us, the more it expands outwards to our loved ones, family, friends, society, and so forth without limits – like the sun that radiates its brilliance throughout the universe. If everyone meditated, the result will be magnified; encircling entire countries and even the whole world. Imagine a world of peace. The police, soldiers and criminal justice system will no longer be necessary when all we feel towards one another is joy and friendship. War, terrorism greed and ignorance are eradicated.

World peace begins with us. It does not require money, international scheme or treaties to execute this plan of peace. It starts by first bringing our mind to a standstill, then spreading it out to the world. Every good thing begins with us when we still our mind in the centre of the body at the seventh base. When our minds are at peace, the process of achieving world peace will not be difficult.

Chapter 5
The Peace Position

To create world peace by allowing one's mind to reach inner happiness first, according to the practice called meditation, is what we ought to do. It is what each and every single person should be concerned with. We should not turn down the opportunity to learn about meditation because of the differences in cultures or beliefs. Although we are born into a particular nationality, religion and race, we are all companions sharing the inevitability of suffering from birth to old age, ailment and death.

Meditation, too, is universal, a practice that everyone can do, like breathing. It helps practitioners improve the quality of their minds by reaching an inner calm and happiness. Meditation relieves stress, giving practitioners mental clarity to tackle problems wisely and allowing them to lead their lives with happiness. These are just the preliminary benefits. Beyond relaxation, there is a distinct feeling of happiness when our minds are resting at the centre. As we become more skilled, there is purity in knowledge that comes from meditation that will help every human being attain his or her inner happiness. The result is wholesome thought, speech and action.

The Most Venerable Phramongkolthepmuni's (Sodh Candasaro) encouragement to practice meditation that teaches us about the seventh base of the mind, along with our own experiences with meditation, shows us how inner happiness can be attained through meditation. The 'Peace Position' is achieved by sitting cross-legged, with the right leg on the left leg, and the right hand on the left hand. While allowing the right index finger to touch the left thumb, sit up straight and maintain awareness.

Then, gently close the eyes and gradually rest the mind at the centre of the body.

Rest the mind at the centre of the body, at the seventh base without analysing, contemplating, or attempting to reason. With regular practice, it will become increasingly easy to bring the mind to the centre of the body or at the centre of the stomach. Ultimately, the mind will become very familiar with this position, which helps to prevent the mind from wandering or drifting.

When the mind is at a standstill and is not distracted or wandering, a deep calmness will be experienced. As the calmness continues, a bright sphere will arise at the centre of the body. This bright sphere is perfectly rounded, translucent and luminous like a crystal ball; like a rain drop. It emerges naturally, representing the purest of the stilled mind at the primary level. It is not a hallucination and neither is it something that is visualised. It has characteristics that are similar to a crystal ball – except that it is brighter and purer. It seems alive. The smallest sphere is about the size of the eye's pupil. At mid-size, the sphere is the size of a full moon; and that of the sun at midday when it is at its largest.

This sphere that arises at the seventh base is the gateway to true happiness and inner peace. It will help us lead a life full of optimism, give us an increasingly purer mind and body, a deeper understanding of life, and ultimately allow us to understand what we need to do in order to attain the highest purpose of our life on earth. This sphere is the initial state of purity that will lead us to an increasing degree of purity that enables us to experience happiness. The deeper we move through each layer, the closer we reach true happiness inside, which is then reflected on the outside. There are so much wonderful possibilities by simply bringing our minds to a standstill at the centre of our bodies. Through this universal meditation practice, we will obtain the answers on our own about the true meaning of peace, where it is located and how we can attain it.

Once we acquire wisdom through meditation, we will come to the same understanding about the futility of wars and weapons of mass destruction. Gone will be the need for hundreds of pages of multilateral written agreements. There will only be people who speak and act honestly. The need to attend the various international peace conferences will lessen, freeing valuable resources for other worthy programmes. Are we ready to embark on this journey together to attain all the benefits of meditation?

As we deepen our inner happiness through meditation, we will start to think, speak and act in harmony because our level of understanding and wisdom will increase. We will understand this when our minds are still. For that reason, a peace prize should be awarded to everyone who has attained inner peace, for they will feel only love and kindness for humanity, and they can be a source of peace for those around them – like a candle illuminating the darkness in the night; like the sun reflecting its warm radiance against other stars, big or small, near or far.

Creating a world filled with happiness through meditation is the noblest of all goals. We need to encourage as many people as possible to practice meditation in their lives, and then spread its wondrous benefits to every corner of the earth. The moment when all the people of the world meditate in this special position – the Peace Position – will be the moment humanity make world peace happen.

Chapter *6*
The Source of Happiness and Peace

The differences among beliefs, cultures, customs, nationalities, religions or languages are only superficial external differences. Beneath these differences, there is a similarity – the original pure nature that exists within everyone. This universal element holds the hope of humanity to bring true peace into the world.

The original pure nature, or the Body of Enlightenment, is a natural state that we can attain when we meditate. The true happiness that we seek is concentrated in the state of pure nature, the inner body that all humanity possesses. It is the origin of happiness, purity and wisdom. It is the centre of all virtues and the source of prosperity of all that is good.

Once attained, the Body of Enlightenment will lead us to true happiness. Our minds will be overflowing with so much happiness and positive energy that one will not want anything else but to remain in the happiness and completeness within. It can be our refuge. It is a happiness that one can experience without reliance on external things like drugs or money. This happiness is different from any mundane happiness obtained from material indulgence.

The Body of Enlightenment, once attained, will lead to justice. The term 'just' means righteous, which is defined as the purest truth. In our pure state, we are all just. Humankind will be united in heart, thought, speech and action. Generosity and fairness will replace greed and selfishness. All the world's limited natural resources will be shared honestly and justly, leading to the total elimination of conflict, poverty and oppression.

Our pure inner nature is as universal as the sun, moon and stars in the sky. If each of us attains a Body of Enlightenment, superficial differences like race, religion and nationality will no longer seem significant or divisive. Brotherly love will blossom and everyone will be a citizen of the world.

Chapter 7

A Treasure
that Cannot
Be Bought

World peace through inner happiness is less costly than any war, and its result is more effective and enduring. Fighting a war requires an immense budget, equipment and the sacrifice of human lives. Conversely, the attaining of inner happiness does not cost us anything. There are no weapons used. It only requires us to defeat the true enemy: the defilements – the root of all suffering, animosity and conflicts of the world. By meditating and concentrating the pure energy within our focused mind at the centre of our body, we can eliminate the defilements. The energy we create is powerful enough to wash away mental blemishes and bring forth a clean, clear and awakened mind. Once our minds are pure, our thoughts, speech and actions will be pure too, and our inner happiness will radiate outwards to our fellowmen and to the world. We will have the strength to abstain from killing, hurting others, stealing, infidelity, lying, drinking, smoking and abusing drugs. When we find our Body of Enlightenment, good moral behaviour will come easily. When the good in us is magnified and the defilements extinguished at the source, wars, anger and hatred will no longer plague humanity.

We each have a role to play in saving the world. Consider this as a very inexpensive investment that requires minimum effort yet yields maximum benefit. We do not have to expend any money. Simply close the eyes gently and relax. Still the mind and good things will come. It is time for us now to join hand in hand to achieve world peace, the most precious treasure of humanity.

Chapter *8*

We Can Change
the World

Peace cannot be achieved through the work of one person or organisation. It requires a concerted effort from everyone. To achieve peace, we will need the participation of every single person. We must share the same vision and work together through a method that is economically realistic with results that are the most beneficial and effective. We just need to close our eyes gently and relax our bodies. We begin by stilling our mind at the centre of our body to generate and focus its strength. World peace begins the moment we each close our eyes to meditate. The strength of the purity from meditating together will spread out and embrace the whole world, destroying the impurities of humanity and banishing the darkness in our minds.

Although we have long dreamed of world peace and of people living together in happiness, we still question whether this dream can ever be a reality. Consider that just 250 years ago, most people would have never imagined that ships could be built from metal and still float; that we could be passengers on planes that fly around the world; that spacecrafts can take us to the moon; or see images of another planet beamed to us from a robot. With the right attempt, even the impossible becomes a concrete reality. Doubts, insecurities and suspicions cannot withstand the sincere efforts of those who seek peace through attaining inner peace. Such people should be our role models in this global movement towards a lasting, all-encompassing peace.

I believe that the dream of a world of enlightenment can be realised in this lifetime. If we do it today, it will happen today. If we do it tomorrow, it will happen tomorrow. If everyone in the world is ready next year, then it will happen next year. If we begin a thousand years from now, it will happen a thousand years from now. When we are committed to the path of enlightenment, there is only a joyous end to our journey.

Testimonies
from Inner Peace
Pioneers

66 The peace starts with me as an individual.
For every individual who comes to meditate
and develops that peace
It means 'another' individual who is out there
who is forming part of what could have been eventually
be a complete body of people
so strong that peace can actually be achieved.
I think there's another wonderful opportunity here
for all the people of South Africa.
It doesn't matter how poor you are.

Meditating is something that doesn't cost you anything
and can change your life.
You can change your life almost overnight.
So, you don't have to worry about
belonging to a religion or a creed.
It doesn't make any difference
if you do belong to a religion or creed.
Meditating cuts across all of those lines
and all it does is provide you
with a wonderful life
with an even better way of practicing your own religion
with a magnificent way of contributing
towards this country
with the most needed thing today – peace.
When I started with meditation here
At the Johannesburg Meditation Centre

I followed the guidelines that were given
This is what I have found very useful
Not having been meditating this way before

Following the little light... the ball of light
which went through the 7th position of the mind
through my body

I follow that step by step
To the centre of my abdomen

Then concentrate on my...
the centre of my being
At that particular point

When I have my mind focused on the centre of my body
And I visualise this light
I try to expand that light
And in the gentlest possible way I concentrate.

It's a need for concentration
And there is a need for relaxation at the same time
So in discovering that balance
I then find that my visualisations change

I feel I get a floating sensation
And a white light that almost dissolves my body
has then been covered in a white light
The actual physical part of my body
Seems to get less and seem to start joining with this light

And that gives me intense peace at that particular time

Then in the process of coming out of it
I think that is very important for me
Is that the feeling I have is carried over
for quite sometime into my life

When I leave the meditation centre
I have that wonderful feeling within me
Something that I would like to share
With other people "

Wren Mast-Ingle
Journalist and consultant (Johannesburg, South Africa)

" Closing my eyes gently and relaxingly, I can feel the moon within because I remember pleasantly walking under the moonlight. As I visualise the image of the moon in my stomach, I feel light as a feather and my inner space filled with happiness. It is unlike owning a Mercedes or a big mansion. Inner happiness is enormous as I visualise the inner moon. After a while, I see the moon in front of me and it moved into my stomach. I simply concentrated with a still mind, and then it 'popped' into the middle of my body.

Before this, I believed that the brain was the most important part for meditation. I'm very happy and delightful to know now that meditation is the true source of real happiness. It creates peace among people – regardless of religions, age or destiny – and it is the universal method that everyone can follow to establish true peace. "

Sultani

46-year-old business owner (Tehran, Iran)

I wish to see everyone in this world practice meditation. It is truly useful. I love Luang Phaw Dhammajayo's saying that "you don't have to pay for meditation". It is wonderful. Meditation simply takes time, attention, love and commitment. Whenever I meditate, I see light that gets brighter and brighter like a sun about the size of a basketball. Finally, I will see a clear crystal sphere at the centre of my body. I have never experienced happiness like this before.

I would like to let everyone know that there is still hope for world peace. The key is to meditate in order to stop the madness and suffering. We have tried wars throughout the different eras, but it's not the solution as it hurts fellow mankind in return.

Following Luang Phaw's teachings is not wrong. I decided to follow his teachings and my life has been totally changed. I think if we all meditate together... being in the same light... sharing the similar happiness... that day would be the day where peace prevails – without the killing, hatred and wars.

Howard McCarry
Entertainer

"I come to meditate here because it makes my mind free. I am feeling quite free in the brain and free inside the spirit, helpful and joyful. My feeling inside my body is I feel enlightened. It's much which cannot express. My feelings before and after meditation are quite different now. Now, I'm different. Before, life was difficult for me. Now I feel free, I feel light. I can solve things quite easily now. I thought my mind was trying too quickly. Now, it's slow. I'd like to recommend meditation to my friends… not only to my friends but to all Black Africans, to all Africans. We grew up not knowing what it is. Now, we grow and we know what it is. And I think it is to prepare us and everyone to bring peace and stability to Africa."

Lucky Moyo

Restaurant Employee (Zimbabwe)

"Just sit quietly being ever so light. Let everything go and it will turn so bright. Seeing yourself for the first time is a wondrous miracle in itself. Imagine you are a diamond Buddha who gives light to the world. You are that already. Through meditation we realise we are all one. Thank you so much my dearest Abbot for all your love that you have given me. You have been my guiding light. You have taught me about the centre of the body, and have always encouraged me to meditate for over the last six years. I love you."

Eric Levine
CEO, California WOW Fitness Center (USA)

“ Meditation teaches you not only to improve your own mental abilities but also to spread kindness and love even to your enemies. Meditation is also a vehicle for finding a peaceful oasis of relaxation and stress relief in a demanding world. Today we live in a very fearful and challenging time. Many people have a concern about their own future due to threats such as nuclear arsenals, terrorism and war. If meditation is practiced throughout the world, such threats can be eliminated by achieving world peace. ”

J.D.A. Wijewardena
Sri Lankan Ambassador to Thailand
Permanent Representative to ESCAP

"Only the happiness we find from the practice of meditation is not changeable. It creates the kind of happiness that is really beneficial to human life. The peace that we gain through meditation is something individual. Individuals make up society. Then each individual has the same reflection towards peace. Peace is something we can have through the development of the mind. What the Abbot is doing is really wonderful and beneficial to the whole world."

Bhante Dhammika
Buddhist Monk (Switzerland)

"What has been a wonderful experience here in this temple is that all religions are welcome. We sit side by side and meditate. The Abbot's vision of world peace through inner peace is absolutely unique. If we find peace within ourselves, we will find peace with each other. It is okay to have different religions but we all live in this world together. The borders between countries should be united, not divided."

Gary Stretch
Hollywood Actor (USA)

"I have tried to show empathy and understanding toward different societies and religions, but empathy has not always been enough. There have been times I have wanted to change hatred to love in other people's mind. I have thus spent enormous energy and words in my arguments. My great Abbot has shown me that true peace is not external; it comes from within. Meditation makes you a good person."

Monica Øien
Program Director and Documentary Maker (Norway)

Sun of Peace

Time for dreaming is over
So reality is now to occur
The world needs no army
Then there be no hostility
When ceasing war in your heart
Disregard the large conference
Gently close both your eyes
Think nothing... sit silencing
None to be committing
Still the mind while relaxing
Imagine a bright sun in your body
Comfortably proceed restfully
Soon we'll be satisfactory
And we'll desire not any
Only love and sympathy
Cherishing joy day and night
World peace from inner bliss
By simple way just like this...

Luang Phaw Dhammajayo
22 March 2006

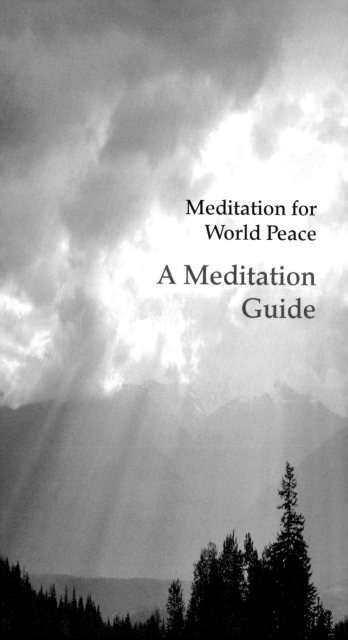

Meditation for
World Peace

A Meditation
Guide

Start by sitting in a relaxed half-lotus position by placing your right leg on your left leg, and your right hand on your left hand. The index finger of your right hand should touch the tip of your left thumb. Place your hands palms up gently on your lap. Sit with your body and head straight. If you cannot sit in this position, you may sit in a chair or on a sofa. Adjust your position so that you feel comfortable, until you feel your breath and circulation flowing freely. Close your eyes gently, just like you are about to fall asleep.

Then take two to three deep breaths. Inhale deeply, feel your stomach expand with air. Exhale slowly. When you are inhaling, let yourself feel

The Seven Bases Leading to Peace of Mind

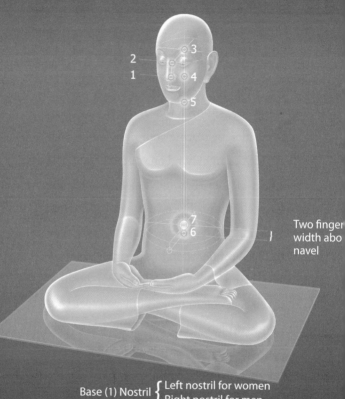

Two finger
width abo
navel

Base (1) Nostril { Left nostril for women / Right nostril for men

Base (2) Bridge of nose { Left for women / Right for men

Base (3) Middle part of head
Base (4) Roof of mouth
Base (5) Throat
Base (6) Navel
Base (7) Centre of gravity

The Seven Bases Leading to Peace of Mind

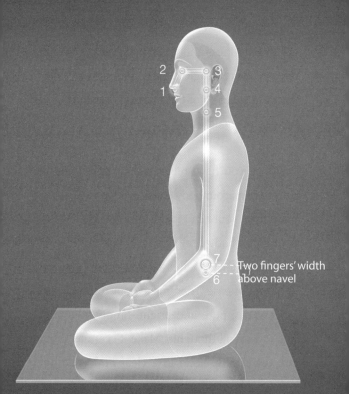

Two fingers' width above navel

Base (1) Nostril { Left nostril for women / Right nostril for men

Base (2) Bridge of nose { Left for women / Right for men

Base (3) Middle part of head
Base (4) Roof of mouth
Base (5) Throat
Base (6) Navel
Base (7) Centre of gravity

as though every cell in your body is attaining the fullest happiness and joy. When you are exhaling, release every single worry and stress. Take a moment to let go of these various concerns. Then breathe normally.

Once you have relieved your mind, you can start to relax your body. Relax every muscle in your body, from your head to the tips of your toes. Relax your entire body at all points. No part of the body should be tense or stressed. You should feel clear, light and at ease. Then make your mind cheerful, fresh, clean, pure and bright. Empty your mind; free it from all thoughts. Make it seem as though you are sitting alone in a clear and wide-open space, a place full of freedom and peace. Imagine that your body is free of internal organs, that it is clear and hollow. You might feel that your body is lighter, now that you have become a part of the atmosphere around you.

Then bring your mind to rest at the centre of the body, in the middle of your stomach, at a level located two finger widths above the navel. It is not necessary to find the exact point. Simply continue to rest your mind gently in the area at the centre of your body. Do this while releasing the tension from your body and your mind.

When you have relaxed your body and mind, start to gently visualise an internal image – that of a clear, perfectly round and unblemished crystal ball. It can be of any size but it should be bright like the midday sun or lucid like a full moon. Visualise it easily and calmly, without forcing the image to arise, without compelling its appearance. If it is not clear, do not be concerned. Whatever appears simply let it occur. And continue to keep your mind calm, still and at rest. If your mind wanders, support yourself with a mantra. Let the sound of the mantra slowly emerge from the middle of the clear crystal ball at the centre of your body. The mantra is "Samma Arahang", which means make the mind pure and detached from all forms of suffering. Or you can use the words "clear and bright". Recite the mantra continuously while calmly observing the crystal ball until your mind becomes still. Then you will stop reciting or naturally forget to recite the mantra. All that will remain is the image of the crystal ball appearing clearly in the centre of your body. Serenely, maintain your concentration to sustain the image, with a mind that is still at all times.

If you have an internal experience that differs from what you normally experience, do not become agitated or excited. Keep your mind unperturbed, just observe dispassionately. Do not be pleased or displeased with what you see. In the end, your mind will become more refined and settle at the centre of your body. Your mind will enter the centre of your body – the point of purity, brightness, true happiness and awareness. This awareness is profound internal wisdom, which grows deeper with continued meditation. You will reach the purity that is found naturally within all of us. This purity is something universal to people across the world.

When your mind is still, there is happiness in your meditation. Before stopping your meditation, perform a loving-kindness meditation. Start by unifying your mind so that it is still and at the centre of your body. Feel that you love others around you and that you want to send good wishes to everyone in the world. Let your mind coalesce into a clear, bright crystal ball that embodies the power of love and good wishes for all living beings. Let this crystal ball expand beyond your body in every direction: right, left, front, back, above and below. Let it spread out in every direction. Let it be a mind that wishes all beings free of suffering and able to attain greater happiness. Wish that all beings will discover the greatest thing: to attain the utmost happiness that arises from meditation and that meditation brings us to the original purity that resides in all of us. You can bring this purity into your daily life. It will make life wholesome and fulfilling, complete with goodness. It will benefit you and others.

Let the crystal ball of your mind expand beyond your body until it surrounds you and others who are both near to and far from you. Let it expand to encompass your present location. Let it grow ever larger until it reaches the sky. Do this until you feel that your mind is boundless and is filled with love and good wishes for your fellow human being on every continent and in every corner of the world.

Let your mind connect with all beings. Let them only have happiness. Let all countries in the world prosper and be full of good people who work for true happiness and peace. Let the power from the purity of your still mind at the centre of your body spread to those people who are suffering because of war. Let their suffering turn into happiness and let this happiness be lasting. Let the people of the world cease exploiting and harming one another. Let people's minds be freed from darkness and become rich in love and compassion.

The energy of purity that comes from meditation is a pure power. This power spreads quietly into the atmosphere. It dispels flaws and darkness in our human minds so they will return to brightness. Let us conduct our lives correctly in happiness with good minds and change the world to achieve true world peace.

Luang Phaw Dhammajayo's Meditation Societies

We welcome you to meditate for peace at our meditation societies located worldwide:

Dhammakaya Temple

**23/2 Mu 7, Khlong Sam, Khlong Luang
Pathum Thani 12120, Thailand
Tel. +(66-2) 831-1000
+(66-2) 524-0257 to 63
Fax. +(66-2) 5240270 to 1
Email : info@dhammakaya.or.th
www.dhammakaya.or.th
www.meditationthai.org
www.dmc.tv/en**

Asia

BRUNEI
Co-ordination Office
Contact: Ruangrassame Chareonying
Tel: +(673) 8-867-029
Email: JY_dhamma@yahoo.com

Thailand Co-ordinator
Contact: Ms. Rawiwon Mechang
Tel: +(66)-5-071-0190

SICHUAN, CHINA
Sichuan Meditation Center
Tel: +(86) 28-8541-8878
+(86) 28-8129-2072
Mobile: +(86) 136-8900-7101
Email: nui072@hotmail.com
pp072@yahoo.com

HONG KONG
The Dhammakaya International Society of Hong Kong Ltd.
385-391, 2/F, Henning House, Hennessy Rd,
Wanchai, Hong Kong
Tel: +(852) 2762-7942
+(852) 2794-7485
Fax: +(852) 2573-2800
Email: dmchk@netvigator.com

IBARAKI, JAPAN
Wat Bhavana Ibaraki
2816-2 Oaza Arakawahongo, Ami-Machi,
Inashiki-gun, Ibaraki-ken, Japan 300-1152
Tel: +(81) 2-9846-6110
Mobile: +(81) 080-5489-5669
+ (81) 080-5489-6659
Email: ibaraki_otera@msn.com

KANAGAWA, JAPAN
Wat Bhavana Kanagawa
3-5-12 Ryosei, Ayase-Shi,Kanagawa-Ken,
252-1126, Japan
Tel: +(81) 4-6770-3264
Mobile: +(81) 90-5099-4527
Email: songtham07@hotmail.com

NAGANO, JAPAN
Wat Thai Nagano
733-3 Mihari, Tomi-Shi, Nagano-Ken,
389-0501, Japan
Tel: +(81) 2-6864-7516
+(81) 2-6864-7720
Fax: +(81) 2-6862-2505
Mobile: +(81) 90-9390-6055
Email: yanakuno@yahoo.com

OSAKA, JAPAN
Dhammakaya International Meditation
Center of Osaka (DIMC of Osaka)
4-6-27 Ohmiya, Asahi-ku, Osaka,
535-0002, Japan
Tel: +(81) 6-6956-1400
Fax: +(81) 6-6956-1401
Email: dimcosaka@hotmail.com

TOCHIGI, JAPAN
Wat Bhavana Tochigi
4-3 Koei-bld. 2F, Demma-Cho, Utsunomiya-shi,
Tochigi-Ken, Japan 320-0035
Tel: +(81) 2-8639-0116
+(81) 0-805-533-9912
Fax: +(81) 2-8614-5663
Email: wattochigi-jp@hotmail.com

TOKYO, JAPAN
Dhammakaya International Meditation
Center of Tokyo
3-78-5 Arakawa, Arakawa-ku, Tokyo,
116-0002, Japan
Tel: +(81) 3-5604-3021
Fax: +(81) 3-5604-3022
Email: chalapinyo@yahoo.com

KUALA LUMPUR, MALAYSIA
Dhammakaya Meditation Center of Kuala Lumpur
7B Jalan, Keannary 4, Bandar Puchong Jaya,
47100, Selangor, Malaysia
Tel: +(60) 3-5882-5887
Mobile: +(60) 17-331-1599
E-mail: dmckl072@yahoo.com

PENANG, MALAYSIA
Dhammakaya Meditation Center of Penang
66, Lengkonk Kenari1, Sungai Ara,
11900 Penang, Malaysia
Tel: +(60) 4-644-1854
Fax: +(60) 19-457-4270 to 1
Email: dmcpn@hotmail.com

SINGAPORE
Kalyanamitta Centre (Singapore)
30 Mohamed Sultan Road #03-00 Lam Ann
Building, Singapore (238974)
Tel: +(65) 6836-1620
Email: info@dhammakaya.org.sg

SOUTH KOREA
Co-ordination Office
Tel: +(83) 10-3040-3299

TAIPEI, TAIWAN R.O.C.
Dhammakaya International Meditation
Center of Taipei
3F No. 9, Lane 16, Sihchuan Rd., Pan-chiao City,
Taipei Country, 22061,Taiwan, R.O.C
Tel: +(886) 2-8966-1000
Fax: +(886) 2-8967-2800
Website: http://dhammakaya.tc

TAOYUAN, TAIWAN R.O.C.
Dhammakaya International Meditation
Center of Taoyuan
No. 232, Ching-Tian Street, Taoyuan City 330
Tel: +(886) 3-377-1261
Mobile: +(886) 9-2252-1072
Email:watthaitaoyuan@hotmail.com

Middle East

BAHRAIN
DMC Centre, Bahrain
1310 Road No. 5641, Block No. 0356,
Manama City, Bahrain
Contact: Mr. Thanachai & Mrs. Peanjai Thongthae
Tel: +(973) 3960-7936
Email: s4p04u@hotmail.com

IRAN
Co-ordination Office
Contact: Ms. Aroona Puenebue
Tel: +(98) 21-2260-2105
Email: marissa_ange@yahoo.com

OMAN
Co-ordination Office
Contact: Ms. Rathanavadee Boonprasert
Tel. +(968) 9901-4584

QATAR
Co-ordination Office
Contact: Ms. Naviya Tonboonrithi
Tel: +(974) 572-7178
Email: naviyatonboonrithi@yahoo.com

SAUDI ARABIA
Co-ordination Office
Contact: Mr. Udom Chimnuan
Tel: +(968) 50-899-1912
Email: saudom_80@yahoo.com

DUBAI
Co-ordination Office
P.O. Box 33084, Dubai, UAE

Contact:
Ms. Sangmanee	Tel: +(971) 50-770-4508
Mr. Methin	Tel: +(971) 50-754-0825
Ms. Dussadee	Tel: +(971) 50-228-5077

THE MIDDLE EAST
Thailand Co-ordinator
Contact: Ms. Rawiwon Mechang
Tel: +(66)-5-071-0190
Email: rawi0072@yahoo.com

Africa

CAPE TOWN
Cape Town Meditation Centre (CMC)
4B Homlfirth Road, Sea Point, Cape Town,
South Africa, 8005
Mobile: +(27) 72-323-0050
+(27) 72-323-0060
+(27) 21-439-1896

JOHANNESBURG
Johannesburg Meditation Centre
30 Scheepers Street, North Riding, Randburg,
Johannesburg, South Africa
Tel: 011-7043360
Mobile: +(27) 79-379-0245
+(27) 73-146-8587
Email: kitsakol@hotmail.com

Europe

ANTWERP, BELGIUM
Dhammakaya International Meditation Centre (Belgium)
Sint-Jobsteenweg 84, 2970'S-Gravenwezel,
Antwerp, Belgium
Tel: +(32) 3.326.45.77 / +(32) 3.289.51.81
Mobile: +(32) 494.32.60.02
Email: vr0072@yahoo.com / vr0072@gmail.com

JUELSMINDE, DENMARK
Wat Buddha Denmark
Gl. Landevej 12, 7130 Juelsminde, Denmark
Tel: +(45) 46.59.00.72
Mobile: +(45) 20.70.74.59
Email: dimc_dk@yahoo.com

BORDEAUX, FRANCE
Wat Bouddha Bordeaux
47, Cours du General de Gaulle,33170
Gradignan, France
Tel: +(33) 5.40.00.93.70
Mobile: +(33) 6.20.23.53.08
Email: pnathi@yahoo.com

PARIS, FRANCE
Wat Bouddha Paris
10, Avenue de Paris, 77164 Ferrieres en Brie,
France
Tel: +(33) 1.64.77.28.37
Fax: +(33) 6.88.25.82.06
Email: vichak@yahoo.com

STRASBOURG, FRANCE
Dhammakaya Centre International de la Meditation
21, Boulevard de Nancy, 67000 Strasbourg, France
Tel: +(33) 3.88.32.69.15
Fax: +(33) 3.88.22.99.19
Email: dimcfr@yahoo.com

AUGSBURG, GERMANY
Wat Buddha Augsburg (Meditation Zentrum)
Pfarrer-Bogner Str.6, 86199 Augsburg, Germany
Tel: +(49) 821.998.3939
Fax: +(49) 821.998.5118
Mobile: +(49) 162.421.0410
Email: ppadec@hotmail.com

FRANKFURT, GERMANY
Wat Buddha Frankfurt (Meditation Verein Frankfurt/Me.V)
Odenwald Str. 22, 65479, Ruanheim, Germany
Tel: +(49) 614.2833.0888
Fax: +(49) 614.2833.0890
Email: lpjon2499@hotmail.com

STUTTGART, GERMANY
Wat Buddha Stuttgart
Im Meissel Str. 6, 71111, Waldenbuch, Germany
Tel: +(49) 715.753.8187
Fax: +(49) 715.753.7677
Mobile: +(49) 16.0179.3782
Email: wat_stuttgart@hotmail.com

BODENSEE, GERMANY
Wat Buddha Bodensee
Lindauer Str 76, 8808 Langenargen
Tel: +(49) 7.4393.9777

MILAN, ITALY
Wat Buddha Milan
Tel: +(39) 30.903.2460
+(39) 33.4338.5849
Fax: +(39) 054.498.7722
Email: fortunebigbank@msn.com
janda.a@hotmail.it

RAVENNA, ITALY
Wat Buddha Italy
Tel: +(39) 348.814.2485
+(39) 338.644.1706
Fax: +(39) 054.498.7722
Email: fortunebigbank@msn.com
janda.a@hotmail.it

MIDNATTSOL, NORWAY
Wat Buddha Midnuttsol
Hvittingfossveien 343, 3080 Holmestrand
Tel: +(47) 33.61.01.43
Fax: +(47) 33.09.66.09
Email: dhammakaya-norway@hotmail.com

GOTHENBÜRG, SWEDEN
Wat Buddha Gothenbürg
Olstorpsvagen 41B, 443 70 Grabo, Sweden
Tel: +(46) 30.24.14.90
Mobile: +(46) 73.75.62.722
Email: pworalert@hotmail.com

SWITZERLAND
Wat Buddha Geneva, Switzerland
Tel: +(41) 796.049.704

LONDON, UNITED KINGDOM
Wat Phra Dhammakaya London
1-2 Brushfield Way, Knaphill, Woking,
GU21 2TG, UK
Tel: +(44) 1483-475757
Fax: +(44) 1483-476161
Mobile: +(44) 7723-351254
Email: disuk@hotmail.co.uk

MANCHESTER, UNITED KINGDOM
Wat Charoenbhavana Manchester
Gardner House, Cheltenham Street, Salford,
Manchester M6 6WY, United Kingdom
Tel: +(44) 161-736-1633
+(44) 798-882-3616
Fax: +(44) 161-736-5747
Email: watmanchester@hotmail.com

North America

CALIFORNIA
Dhammakaya International Meditation Center (USA)
801 E. Foothill Blvd., Azusa, CA 91702 USA
Tel: +(1)-626-334-2160
Fax: +(1)-626-334-0702
Email: dimcazusa@yahoo.com

FLORIDA
Florida Meditation Center
1303 N. Gordon St, Plant City, FL 33563 USA
Tel: +(1)-813-719-8000
+(1)-813-719-8005
Fax: +(1)-813-719-8007
Email: pamotito@msn.com

GEORGIA
Georgia Meditation Center Inc.
12250 King Cir., Roswell, GA 30075 USA
Tel: +(1)-770-643-1233
Fax: +(1)-770-643-9756
Email: somboonusa@yahoo.com

ILLINOIS
Meditation Center of Chicago (M.C.C.)
6224 W. Gunnison St., Chicago, IL 60630 USA
Tel: +(1)-773-763-8763
Fax: +(1)-773-763-7897
Email: Mcc_072@yahoo.com

MINNESOTA
Minnesota Meditation Center
242 Northdale Blvd NW, Coon Rapids, MN 55448
USA
Tel: +(1)-763-862-6122
Fax: +(1)-763-862-6123
Email: MMC_072@yahoo.com

NEW JERSEY
Dhammakaya International Meditation Center of New Jersey
257 Midway Ave., Fanwood, NJ 07023 USA
Tel: +(1)-908-322-4187
+(1)-908-322-4032
Fax: +(1)-908-322-1397
Email: dimc_nj@yahoo.com

OREGON
Oregon Meditation Center
13208 SE. Stark Street, Portland, OR 97233 USA
Tel: +(1)-503-252-3637
Mobile: +(1)-503-799-8547
Email: omc072@yahoo.com

TEXAS
Meditation Center of Texas
1011 Thannisch Dr., Arlington, TX 76011 USA
Tel: +(1)-817-275-7700
Email: asabha072@hotmail.com

WASHINGTON
Seattle Meditation Center
852 N.E. 83rd Street Seattle, WA 98115 USA
Tel: +(1)-206-522-1514
Fax: +(1)-206-985-2920
Email: mahasamma@hotmail.com

VIRGINIA
Meditation Center of D.C.
3325 Franconia Rd., Alexandria, VA 22310 USA
Tel: +(1)-703-329-0350
Fax: +(1)-703-329-0062
Email: pratyanj@hotmail.com

OTTAWA, CANADA
Co-ordination Office
354 Breckenridge Cres. Ottawa,
Ontario K2W1J4, Canada
Contact: Pattrawan Sukantha
Tel: +(613) 254-9809
+(613) 261-4341
Email: jayy.dee@hotmail.com

MONTREAL, CANADA
Co-ordination Office
3431 Jeanne-Manae Suite #8,
Quebec H2x2J7, Canada
Contact: Gritsana Sujjinanont
Tel: +(514) 845-5002
+(514)726-1639
Email: gritsana@netzero.net

TORONTO, CANADA
Contact: Pipat Sripimolphan
Tel: +(647) 886-0347
Email: psripimolphan@yahoo.com

Oceania

SYDNEY RETREAT
Wat Phra Dhammakaya, Sydney
Lot 3, Inspiration Place, Berrilee, NSW 2159
Tel: +(61) 2-9655-1128
Fax: +(61) 2-9655-1129
Mobile: +(61) 4-1162-8677
Email: Satit@dhammakaya.org.au

SYDNEY OFFICE
Dhammakaya Meditation Centre
(Sydney Office)
117 Homebush Rd, Strathfield NSW 2135,
Australia
Tel: +(61) 2-9742-3031
Fax: +(61) 2-9742-3431
Mobile: +(61) 4-1145-3946

BRISBANE
Brisbane Meditation Centre
73 Lodge Rd., Wooloowin QLD 4030, Australia
Tel: +(61) 7-3857-3431
Mobile: +(61) 4-3105-7215

MELBOURNE
Dhammakaya Meditation Centre of Melbourne
84 Oakwood Rd., St. Albans 3021, Australia
Tel: +(61) 3-9266-0181
Mobile: +(61) 4-0100-8799
Email: ronrawee@yahoo.com.au

PERTH
Dhammakaya Meditation Centre of Perth
174 Moolanda Boulevard, Kingsley,WA, 6026,
Australia
Tel: +(61) 8-9409-8614
Mobile: +(61) 4-302-07877
Email: phra_tawee@yahoo.com.au

OREWA
Orewa Meditation Centre
43 Albatross Road, Red Beach,HBC, Auckland,
New Zealand, 1461
Tel: +(64) 9-427-4263
Fax: +(64) 9-427-4264
Mobile: +(64) 21-153-8592
Email: orewameditation@yahoo.com.au

DUNEDIN
Dunedin Meditation Centre (DDMC)
10 Barnes Drive, Caversham, Dunedin ,
New Zealand, 9001
Tel: +(64) 3-487-6772
Fax: +(64) 3-487-6775
Mobile: +(64) 2-199-3780
Email: thep072@yahoo.com

SOLOMON ISLANDS
Co-ordination Office
KITANO WKK JV P.O.BOX 1108 Honiara
Solomon Islands
Contact: Mr. Sangwian Khanchaiyaphum
Tel: +(677) 24808
Fax: +(677) 25460
Email: peleyo3@hotmail.com

Luang Phaw Dhammajayo

Luang Phaw Dhammajayo (The Most Venerable Phrarajbhavanavisudh) was born in 1944 at Singburi Province, Thailand. His interests in Buddhism and meditation began when he was still in his adolescence. After graduating with a Bachelor's degree, he was ordained as a Buddhist monk at the age of 25 at Wat Paknam Bhasichareon.

In 1970, Venerable Dhammajayo and his community established the Buddhachakka Meditation Centre (Soon Buddhacak-Patipatthamm) in Pathumthani Province, Thailand. It later developed into the Dhammakaya Temple which provides activities that are very beneficial to the society. Venerable Dhammajayo has also received an Honorary Doctorate Degree in Buddhist Studies from the Maha Chulalongkorn Raja Vidhayalai University.

He was the first Thai Buddhist monk to receive the Mahatma Gandhi Peace Award from the All Indian Gandhian Worker Society, India, in 2005. He also received the Universal Peace Award from the World Buddhist Sangha Youth, Sri Lanka, in 2006. He is an individual who has devoted himself to creating world peace through inner peace employing meditation to bridge the differences between people of different countries, religions and nationalities to attain the Dhammakaya within and to teach ethics to the general public – within Thailand and over 60 countries around the world.

Venerable Dhammajayo's Dhamma programme is broadcast through the DMC (Dhamma Media Channel) Satellite and the Internet (www.dmc.tv/en). The programme is available in Thai, English and Chinese languages to continents around the world.

Live Meditation Lessons

The Dhammakaya Foundation offers meditation lessons on a satellite TV channel called DMC, run by its affiliated organisation. The channel provides 24-hour coverage on meditation, Dhamma talks, news, music, health programmes, children's and youth's programmes in the Thai language. Viewing is completely free of charge.

A select number of programmes are available in English, Chinese, Japanese, Vietnamese, German and Spanish. English-language programmes include a live meditation lesson at 0700-0730 GMT (1200-1230 ET) on Tuesdays through Sundays and Meditation for All, a feature programme broadcast at 2200-2230 GMT (1600-1630 ET) every Sunday. You can join a live mass meditation session at 1640-1800 and 2030-2100 GMT on Sundays. A case study-based Dhamma programme with English subtitles is available Monday through Saturday at 0230-0300 GMT (0040-0110 ET).

You can watch the programmes on the satellite TV or on **www.dmc.tv/en**.

Tomorrow the World Will Change

Honorary Consultants:
Phrarajbhavanavisudh (Ven. Dhammajayo Bhikkhu)
Phrabhavanaviriyakhun (Ven. Dattajeevo Bhikkhu)

Consultants:
Ven.Chatchai Chattanchayo
Ven.Amnuaysak Munisakko
Ven.Sombat Rakkitajitto
Ven.Ronnapob Jotilabho
Anant Asavabhokhin
Boonchai Bencharongkul
Prakob Chirakiti (Ph.D)
Vanna Chirakiti
Metta Suvachitvong

Executive Editors:
Ven. Sanchaya Nakajayo
Supakij Nantarojanaporn
Peter Wong

Editors:
Aaron Stern (Ph.D)
Chanida Jantrasrisalai
Jeff Wilson (Ph.D)
Jennifer Kitil Jenarewong
Jo-Ann Sainz (Ph.D)
Lucille Klucklas
Narongchai Saenmahayak
Paul Trafford (Ph.D)
Siriporn Sirikwanchai (Ph.D)
Suparat Vinaiwat
Walailuck Mongkolkawil

Rewriters:
Sarinee Vorasubin
Marc Hubbard
The Print Lodge Pte Ltd

Translators:
Anchalee Stern
Jarin Kamphonphanitwong
Manikanto Bhikkhu
Panadda Thanasuansan
Phatara Inlarp
Richard Timer
Sarinratana Sukhabutr
Shinavit Sukhawat
Sith Chaisurote
Suganda Cluver
Supanee Kude
Supichaya Panprasert
Tawatchai Petchsingto
Thiranop Wangkijchinda
Veerachart Siriwattanapat
Waraporn Chettabudr
Wiwat Kamolpornwijit (Ph.D)
Worawit Siriwattanapat

Coordinators:
Wichaya Triwichien and Team